A CHRISTIAN W

OVERCOMING

Messy

EMOTIONS

To:
Tanya
Thank you!
D. George
Psalm 20:4

BY DR. GEORGIA POINTER

An Encouragement Outpost Book

ISBN: 979-8-9854130-0-7 (print)

ISBN: 979-8-9854130-1-4 (ebook)

Library of Congress Control Number: 2022901755

This edition independently published by Author Georgia Pointer.

Contact: ordinerrygirl@yahoo.com

Website: www.encouragementoutpost.com

Editorial Services by Kelsy Jelinek Editorial (kelsey.jelinek@gmail.com)

Design Edits by Laura Rivera-Rexach (contact@designsxlaura.com)

Publication Services by 3Trees Publishing (3treespublishing@gmail.com)

Contents

A Christian Woman's Guide To Overcoming Messy Emotions

Dr. Georgia Pointer

An Encouragement Outpost Book

Acknowledgments

To my beloved Keith, thank you for everything you have done to support the writing of this book. You are the wind beneath my wings. To Janet and Charlana, thank you so much for your encouragement and willingness to share what God has given you. Because of your faith in me, I believe the best is yet to come. To Sara and Christine, thank you for your prayers and encouragement. They have meant more than you know. To Jessica, thank you for your belief that helped my unbelief so many times. To Kelsy, thank you for making me look like I know what I am doing. Your expertise is much appreciated.

To my beloved Savior, Jesus Christ, thank You so much for your beautiful invasion into the life of a timid, insecure, and hurting 13-year-old-girl all those year ago. May this book be a sweet offering of gratitude for all the healing you have done in me. Let many be helped and encouraged by this book. May every healing be another crown thrown at Your feet.

Preface

Do you ever feel emotions you do not want to feel? You are jealous of a friends' good fortune. You are angry but try to act as though you are not. You encounter someone who did you wrong years ago, and those ugly feelings come back. You are happy that someone who always seems to win finally loses. These are what I call messy emotions, and we all have them. As a Christian, you want to love the Lord with all your mind, but it keeps filling up with thoughts that do not reflect Christ's love and purity. If you are like me, you try to muster up the strength to feel the right way, but it only gets worse. You confess and repent and think you are doing better only to find those emotions grow back like mold.

If a foul odor in your kitchen assaults your nostrils and you only spray perfume around, have you handled the problem? No. You must get rid of the source of the problem and then the smell will go away too. The same is true of your messy emotions. They do not exist in isolation. You may try to will your bad feelings away. You may ignore them. Maybe you deny they are there because you are ashamed of them. You may justify why those feelings have the right to be there. All this is just perfume, my friend. Again, your emotions do not exist in isolation. They are connected to beliefs and thoughts you may not even realize you have. Left unattended, these unpleasant or troubling feelings can affect relationships, hinder ministry, or become strongholds. Messy emotions provide an opportunity for growth in your relationship with God and with others. Tackling them can be difficult, but the effort is well worth it.

If you keep in mind two truths, this journey can be a fruitful and encouraging one. First, remember that God loves you and wants to bring about healing and change. Because the Lord is a God of grace, recognize that any condemnation you may sense when reading this book is from the enemy of your soul, the devil himself. Condemnation is always from the devil. Conviction, on the other hand, is from the Lord. Condemnation says there is no hope for you, but conviction shows your wrong so that you may correct it and move forward. Secondly, remember that God's truth is greater than your emotions. Jesus prayed you would be sanctified by God's truth, and then He clarified that God's Word is truth (John 17:17). Your emotions are not the boss of you. God's truth is. As a Christian, you have a new nature in Christ, but the flesh is still putting up a fight. I encourage you to pray as you read this book. Ask God to show you what He sees that needs correction. Ask Him to then show you how to become more like Him.

If you have entered a personal relationship with God through salvation in Jesus Christ, you have what it takes to overcome your messy emotions. If you have not yet entered a personal relationship with Christ, you can today. Please see the index on page 53 of this book. You have the mind of Christ, but the mind of the flesh keeps trying to crowd it. The Person of the Holy Spirit lives inside you, and with Him comes all the power you need "for life and godliness" (2 Peter 1:3). Like the apostle Paul, you have the same right to say, "I have been crucified with Christ and I no longer live, but Christ lives in me. The life I now live in the body, I live by faith in the Son of God, who loved me and gave himself for me," (Galatians 2:20). This book will show you how to look beneath the "smell" of your messy emotions and deal with the source of them. The result will be new insight into yourself, a fresh appreciation for the grace of God, and greater victory in the ongoing battle of your thoughts and emotions. This book will provoke you to invite God into areas of your life you do not realize are closed.

Please resist the temptation to rush through this book. Each chapter will provide space to write what you are processing. If you need to, you may start a journal to help you work through what lies beneath your messy emotions. I encourage you to pause and dialogue with God and yourself about what you read. Our culture is always in a hurry to fix things. My husband says I am the most impatient woman he knows, so I understand the struggle. Emotional health is a journey that deserves time to ask honest questions and then ponder long enough to produce good answers.

Fear

I WAS A CHICKEN. As a child, I was afraid of dogs, the dark, and anyone who wanted to fight. Everybody seemed to want to fight. My mama said if I stood up to my bullies, they would leave me alone. I never did. I tried to outrun them. I was so afraid of a particular bully that I peed in my pants every day for months to get away from her. Why did I do this? I reasoned if I stopped to go to the bathroom before leaving for home, I would waste valuable seconds getting ahead of my bully after seventh period. I was never able to hold it all the way home. Hours since lunchtime, all that hard running made it impossible to keep it in, so I wound up peeing my pants.-My mother never knew. I threw everything in the wash before she arrived home.

I wanted to be a cheerleader but was afraid I would fail, so I never tried out. I was afraid to be myself because people might reject me, so I kept to myself. Fear saturated my life. God has done a lot of work in me since then, but even now fear still has some hiding places in my heart. Despite the fear, I have too much I want to do in my life to let it stop me. I hope this is true for you, too.

To be human is to experience fear. Fear serves as an alert to protect yourself from danger. Other times, fear hinders. What are you afraid of? Missing out? What others think of you? The future? When these fears control you, you live beneath your privilege as a child of God. "God has not given us a spirit of fear, but of power, of love and of a sound mind" (2 Timothy 1:7). The moment a person surrenders to Christ and receives his gift of salvation, God places his Holy Spirit inside that new believer (John 15:26; Romans 8:8-9). If you have received him, his Spirit is alive in you and can empower you to face your fears and overcome them. What can you do to overcome fear? What truths must you keep in mind to remind you of God's power?

Know That God Is with You

The most effective truth in overcoming fear is the knowledge that God is with you. This means you are never outnumbered, my friend. You, plus God, makes a winning combination. The moment you receive Christ, His Spirit enters your heart with a promise to be a permanent resident, and He brings all the benefits of that union with Him (Hebrews 13:5). As Creator of the universe, He brought His authority and power with Him (John 1:3). Union with Christ opens amazing possibilities and privileges for you. You have more at your disposal than you will ever need.

I love the account in 2 Kings 6 when Elisha's servant came in screaming that an enemy army had surrounded the house. Who would stay calm at a time like that? A person who sees what cannot be seen with natural eyes. That is who! Elisha calmly asked the Lord to show the servant why panic was unnecessary. Then God opened the servant's eyes to see a host of horses and chariots of fire surrounding the enemy army.

What does this Old Testament story have to do with your modern-day fear? In Christ, God is on your side, my friend. You already have the victory. Forge ahead despite what fear is telling you. You may not see the angel army surrounding your enemies; you need to trust it is there and act accordingly.

How does knowing God is with you help to overcome fear? It works when you remind yourself who God is and what He can do. One of the lies fear tells is that everything is up to you. Fear ridicules you and points to all your weaknesses, distracting you from the call of God on your life. It never lets you forget all the times you failed. For this reason, you must treat fear like a bully. Fear is like an atheist. It denies the existence or care of God in your situation. Interrupt its lies with God's truth. Christ tells you that apart from Him you can do nothing (John 15:5). He says you can do all things through Him because He will give you strength (Philippians 4:13). He also promises He will never leave you nor forsake you (Hebrews 13:5). These truths were not only meant for Gideon and his tiny army (Judges 6-8) or Daniel in the lion's den (Daniel 6). They are meant for you in your fearful circumstances. Do not fall for the lie that your problems are small compared to fighting off an army or bearing the anger of a national leader. If it is big enough to make you afraid, then it matters to God. That is why He assures you of His presence, so you can call on Him in those moments. Fear insists you focus on yourself and your limitations. Trust in God's power allows you to see past your limitations and overcome.

Take Courage

Another weapon in your fight against fear is courage. Again, it is not based on believing in yourself. Its foundation is built upon God's strength working through you. You cannot have courage without taking action to combat your fear. Sometimes we quote verses about being overcomers, but never venture to do the work of overcoming. Courage means to act. For example, you are afraid of the boss who intimidates you at work. You allow him to humiliate you in front of your coworkers or intimidate you. What does it look like to face this fear with action? Can you schedule a meeting and respectfully confront your boss about his rudeness? Can you say "no" to his request to lie on a sales report? Messy emotions like fear are fueled by false beliefs. What belief might be fueling your fear of your boss? Perhaps, you believe there is no choice but to let him bully you. He pays your salary, and you might get fired, so you put up with the abuse. Maybe you believe the lie that somehow you deserve that kind of treatment. It is not always easy to pinpoint the lies that hid behind your fear. Pray what the palmist prayed, "Search me, God, and know my heart; test me and know my anxious thoughts. See if there is any offensive way in me and lead me in the way everlasting" (Psalm 139:23-24).

Once you discern the lie, counteract it with the truth. If the lie is that you have no choice but to take the abuse, then what truth does God want you to remember? Perhaps the courageous action you should take is to find another job. God does not call you to avoid challenging situations. However, do not allow abuse to continue because you are afraid to speak up.

Determine that you will not allow fear to rule you. Do not let it keep you from moving forward, even if you shake with every step.

Do It Anyway

Sometimes fear goes away at the first sign of God's truth.

Other times you must apply more spiritual muscle. When fear puts up a fight, arm yourself with a prayer on your lips and a verse of Scripture in your mind.

Fear may do its worst, but you will still do your best. If you supply the willingness, God will supply the power! You may be thinking, "I do not even have the willingness." No worries, my friend. According to Philippians 2:13, God can supply even that! Surrender your will to Him like a glove to a hand. He will do things through you that will stop fear in its tracks.

Enlist Accountability

A final weapon in your war against fear is accountability. You were never meant to face fear alone. Yes, God is always with you, but He also equips you with helpers. Find friends who share your commitment to Christ and enlist their support to face your fear. In Proverbs 27:17 it is written, "As iron sharpens iron, so one person sharpens another." Who can you call on to pray for you and support you in the fight against fear?

Reflections

1. What is your biggest fear?

2. How have you tried to overcome fear in the past? Has it worked?

3. Of the ways listed above, which are you most excited to try?

. . .

4. Who will you trust to be your accountability partner in your journey to overcome your fears?

5. What specific action will you take TODAY to work toward overcoming fear?

Devastation and Brokenness

A TORNADO RIPS through everything in your town.
Someone steals your identity and ruins you financially. A rape
changes you and your family forever. The death of someone
you love darkens your days. A terminal diagnosis shatters you.
A betrayal cuts you deep, and you struggle to trust anyone
again.

Trauma, devastation, and brokenness are never what any
of us want. Life has a way of blindsiding and leaving us
reeling in disbelief. Time can heal, yes, but what do you do
until it does? It is important to hold onto the One who never
changes. Your emotions go in many different directions, like a
rabid Tasmanian devil. You cannot trust them to guide you in
dark times. You must have an anchor dropped to keep you
from getting lost in your despair. What I am about to share
may seem too simple to work, but simple is what you will need
in desperate times.

You are not alone

First, you must remember you are not alone in your distress. It is written in Psalm 34:18, "The Lord is close to the brokenhearted and saves those who are crushed in spirit." Your circumstances may tempt you to assume God has forsaken you, but they are lying. This will be a time that tests your faith. God is there even when you cannot see Him or feel Him. His presence is a fact that never changes. Be careful about trying to figure out the "whys." This may not be the time for that. This is the time to trust. God is here. Talk to Him. Be honest about what you are thinking and feeling. You may swing from anger to doubt to fear to faith and back again. The room of suffering has messy emotions splattered all over it. Your vulnerabilities come out of the dark when you are broken. Express these to God so He can speak the truth back to you. In all your expressions, never lose respect for the Almighty. You can tell God you feel He is being unfair. However, be wise to remember this is not true, even if it is how you feel. Ask God to show you when your views are wrong. This is no different than any other issue of struggle. Ask Him for the perspective you need to get through it.

Find a Healthy Outlet

Find a healthy way to process your emotions. Try journaling or talking with a friend or family member. It is best if you have more than one person to help you through this time. It might be easier to communicate your feelings in a support group than with people who are close to you. Feel free to express your emotions creatively, through whatever medium you prefer. Painting, playing a musical instrument, or working with clay are a few examples.

. . .

Heal through Service to Others

At some point, you may find serving others is a great way to take your mind off your own troubles. Volunteering often turns out to be more help to you than the people you serve. It helps put your troubles into perspective. You recognize you are not the only one who has suffered. You may find helping others to be the therapy your spirit needs.

You Can Grow from This

Job is a Bible character who experienced more devastation than most. He lost all his children, crops, and health in one day. His faith stayed strong because he had the right perspective about his possessions. His children were dead, yes, but he had comfort knowing he would see them again. Despite his strong faith, Job still had room to grow. We all do. While trials are not always a punishment, they always serve to purify. Job's suffering brought out some impurities he did not know he had. Yours will too. There is nothing like seeing what suffering exposes in you to make you appreciate God's eternal grace. Devastation is humbling because it reminds us how little control we have over our lives. Even more humbling is the person it reveals as we grapple with hurt, inconvenience, disillusionment, need, and wounded pride.

It is appropriate and healthy to grieve. Oh, but God says we are not to "grieve like the rest of mankind, who have no hope" (1 Thessalonians 4:13). Work through anger, disillusionment, and pain. Bring every bit of it to Jesus and allow Him to carry you through your struggle. Look at your situation in all its ugliness and know God will bring something beautiful from it. Also, God changes you! Distress and devastation are often the tools God uses to conform you to Christlikeness. No, it is not what you would choose, but it is what you and I need.

Trust God is good even when He allows you experience pain. He never says you will escape heartache or trouble. He promises you never have to face it alone.

Your growth is God's intent, but you must surrender to it. Tough times make you bitter if you let them. Acknowledge your need for God at this vulnerable time in your relationship with Him. Bitterness, a weed stemming from the root of entitlement, blocks the growth you need to blossom into the person who overcomes trials with maturity. "And we know that in all things God works for the good of those who live him, who have been called according to his purpose," (Romans 8:28). You might not want to hear that right now, but it is the truth you need. Know that God is up to something good, my friend. Let your heart believe this, even when you cannot feel it.

Reflections

1. What has you feeling broken today, my friend? Name it here.

2. List all the messy emotions this terrible time has squeezed out of you. You can be honest; God knows about them already anyway.

3. What attributes of God do you need to remember most at this difficult time?

4. God is near to the brokenhearted (Psalm 34:18). Write a prayer of faith and trust to God below. Even if your heart

does not feel the way you wish it did, write what you need God to help your heart believe.

5. What healthy outlets can you use to work through your grief or heartbreak?

6. Over time, you will see the growth God brings. When you are ready, celebrate that growth by writing about it below.

3

Unforgiveness

THE TENSION between Joseph and his brothers had been
mounting since the day their father, Jacob, gifted him with the
colorful coat. He was having dreams he just had to share with
someone. His brothers seemed the appropriate audience, but
the more he shared the dreams, the more antagonistic and
hateful they became. One morning, his brothers went out to
tend the flocks. Their father sent Joseph to bring back a report
on how they were doing. The morning chill provided an
ample excuse to put on his prized coat while he went out to
fulfill his father's errand. Joseph could not find his siblings at
the usual spot. After asking a man if he had seen them, Joseph
headed to Dothan. In the distance, he saw the collective
silhouettes of his brothers crowded together around a fire.
From there, he could not see the hateful scowls on their faces.
Nor could he hear the slurs about him seething through their
angry teeth. Finally, close enough to make out their faces, they
suddenly charged him at once, ripping his coat off with such
violence he had burns where the fabric scraped his skin.
Shouting for them to stop, Joseph sustained further injury as
they raked him across the rocky ground. Hurled into the pit,

he heard laughter laced with rage as his assailants sat close by eating lunch. Screaming and begging until his throat grew raw and hoarse, Joseph's dreams never told him what nightmares lay ahead.

You know how the rest of the story went. Joseph was sold into slavery, falsely accused of sexual assault, and forgotten by the one who owed him a favor. He had every opportunity to let a poisonous weed of bitterness grow in his heart. Believing God's promise that he would one day rule in Egypt, Joseph could have consoled himself with dreams of vengeance. Joseph suffered for such a long time, yet when he had the opportunity to get back at his brothers, he had a supernatural perspective and response (Genesis 37-50).

You can have one too!

What is your story? Who has betrayed you, stolen your innocence, harmed someone you love, or ruined you financially? How long is your list of hurts? How long has your bitterness festered, my friend? What good has rehearsing those hurts done you? Even if you cannot see it, unforgiveness is hindering you. God says there is a connection between His forgiveness of you and your forgiveness of others (1 John 4:19, Ephesians 4:32).

You have tried to forgive but failed. Just when you think you have forgiven, something happens, and your hurt or anger comes back.

How do you forgive what seems unforgiveable?

The answer may surprise you. Forgiveness begins with recognizing you already possess forgiveness. You just haven't activated it. As a blood-bought, Holy Spirit-infused and empowered follower of Jesus Christ, you possess the ability to forgive even before the desire to forgive happens. "His divine power has given us everything we need for a godly life," (2 Peter 1:3). This includes the ability to forgive. Forgiveness is a fruit of the Spirit. No, you do not see it listed in Galatians

5:22-23, but it is there in the word "love." What does love do if it does not forgive? Love "keeps no record of wrongs," but unforgiveness does (1 Corinthians 1:5). Love is humble, but unforgiveness is arrogant. It holds a grudge in one hand while receiving God's grace for its own sins in the other. "Love is kind" but unforgiveness is rude, forgetting its manners (1Corinthians 13:4). "Love is patient" (1 Corinthians 13:4). Unforgiveness says its offender has used up all the chances to make amends. Love and forgiveness sound impossible.

They are... in your own strength. It is a good thing it is not all up to you to muster the needed grace and power to forgive. Christ enables you to forgive.

Here is another surprise: Forgiveness has almost nothing to do with your offender. The main characters in your forgiveness story are you and God. Look at the story Jesus told in Matthew 18:23-25. A king forgave a man a huge debt he could never repay. The man found someone who owed him far less money. Notice the pleading words are almost identical to the ones the king heard. Sadly, the first debtor refused to extend the same grace he received. The king heard about this and called the man back, exacting severe judgment. You would think it was none of the king's business how his servant treated the other man. Notice the severe judgment came because of the first debtor's lack of mercy. Jesus was illustrating that your lack of forgiveness toward others is His business. God says because He has forgiven you far more than anyone could ever owe you, you owe it to *Him* to forgive your offender. It is His divine right to interfere. It is your divine responsibility to forgive, not because your offender deserves it, but because of the forgive-ness God gave you. When you imprison your offender through unforgiveness, you imprison yourself too. It is all connected. This means you exercise forgiveness by taking your eyes off your offender and focusing them on the magnitude of God's mercy. Quit itemizing their faults and failures, my friend, and begin confessing your own sins to God. Can you calculate how many times He has wiped your guilty slate clean? The result will be humility, grace, and yes, forgiveness.

Every time the fumes of unforgiveness start to fill the air, attack the source with the sweet-smelling grace of God. When the scab gets scraped off old hurts, apply the balm of His mercy, and the healing will begin again.

Forgiving can feel like the other person gets away with something. If you do not get back at them, you feel vulnerable to their ridicule and to repeat offenses. God is not mocked, my friend. Just as your unforgiveness is between you and God, their offense against you is between them and God. He does not need you to fight His battles. Leave your offender to Him (Romans 12:19). If they choose not to seek God's forgiveness, they will wish you had dealt with them instead of the Almighty. Forgiving your offender frees you, but it does not release your offender from the consequences of their offenses toward you.

What forgiveness Is Not

Yes, forgiveness is a decision you have the power to make through the Holy Spirit. Yes, forgiveness is your response to others because of the grace of God in your own life.

Forgiveness Is Not a Feeling

Forgiveness is a choice, not a feeling. You may never have gushy or fuzzy feelings toward the person you forgive, but you can decide how you will behave toward them. This is rudimentary self-control, my friend. You do it all the time in other areas of your life. You do not feel like paying your bills, taking out the trash, respecting your horrible boss, exercising, or getting up early to go to work. You do them because you know you need to, and it is part of being a responsible adult. Forgiveness is not any different. You set your mind on what God did for you and in obedience you do what you do not feel like doing. It is a commandment to obey, and your feelings do not get a say in it.

Forgiveness Is Not Living Without Boundaries -Proverbs 22:3

You can forgive your offenders without allowing them back into your life. They must earn back the trust they lost with you. You can decide that too much damage has been done and you are not comfortable having them occupy the same space in your heart or life they once did. Forgiveness does not mean everything has to go back to the way it was before. Actions have consequences, even in the face of forgiveness.

Forgiveness Is Not Excusing What They Did -Galatians 6:7

Forgiveness is not excusing what your offender did. Wrong is whatever God says it is. It is not denying or relabeling what they did to you. Forgiveness must operate in the face of the truth of the offense, otherwise how can you know what you are forgiving? How will you know what you do not want to happen again?

Forgiveness Is Not Weakness- Proverbs 19:11; 16:22

Forgiveness is not weakness. It often takes more strength to forgive than to enact vengeance. Anybody can pay back wrong for wrong. It requires strength and control to forgive. There is nothing weak about it!

Forgiving Yourself

Some people may believe that forgiving yourself is nowhere in the Bible. They say we love ourselves to the point of selfishness, so forgiving ourselves is something we are prone to do anyway. I disagree. Lots of other people have a tough time loving themselves. You may be one of them. You may struggle to ignore the voices from your past that have attacked your identity and worth. You may find it difficult to extend grace to yourself due to perfectionism. Past failures may haunt you and cripple you from moving forward. The Bible verses that speak of forgiveness also apply to forgiving yourself. I say this because the reason for forgiveness always points to the grace of God. For example, Ephesians 4:32 says, "Be kind and compassionate to one another, forgiving each other, just as in Christ God forgave you." The foundation for forgiveness is that through Christ, God forgives you. This is the same foundation on which self-forgiveness stands. You forgive yourself because Christ forgives you. To be unforgiving to yourself is to hold a grudge against someone God declares forgiven. God has an issue with your unforgiveness of yourself as much as He does when you hold a grudge against someone else. It is about respecting and accepting the work Christ did on the cross to secure forgiveness for you. When you do not forgive yourself, you insult the blood of Christ by implying it is not enough to cover your sin. You may feel you do not deserve forgiveness, and you are right. That is what makes forgiveness so beautiful! It is about grace and mercy, not deserving. So, forgive yourself today as a decision and an act of obedience to God. Do it out of respect for the great price Christ paid for you to have it, my friend.

Reflections

Everyone one has somebody who has done them wrong. You may have a long list, or just a few people. They keep doing the same wrong to you over and over. Either way, for your own good, you must forgive. I have discovered that forgiveness is decision you make over and over. By God's grace, you start with the initial decision, and then remind your emotions of that fact every time they flare up. Focus on God's grace toward you and leave your offender to God. In case you need to do it or do it again, here is the space for it:

"God, thank you for the full and free forgiveness when I ...

"God, I extend that same forgiveness to my offender(s)." (You might not want to write their name here, but you can breathe their name into this spot on the page so that your flesh will know you mean business.)

4

Anger

ALL ANGER IS NOT SINFUL. Some anger is righteous. All anger must be controlled. You can be victorious in controlling your anger, my friend. God has given you His Spirit and a fruit of His Spirit is self-control (Galatians 5:23).

I told a friend that I was writing this book and would address anger. She growled, squirmed, and said I should leave angry people alone and write to the folks always causing the anger. She confessed she struggles with anger most days. I had a feeling she did, though it was not as obvious as another woman I remember. She seemed always to talk loudly to people and to be suspicious of everyone. It was as though she feared someone was out to take advantage of her. She wanted everyone to know she was tough. She had a gruff and blunt way of speaking to people. I often wondered who hurt her and caused her to think she needed to have the upper hand in every relationship. She argued a lot with the people around her. It seemed important to her to have the last word in every argument. Sinful anger usually has a backstory. It often is a clue that some pain in the past has not been healed. If you struggle with anger, I encourage you to ask God to help you deal with the underlying pain so that you can heal and be free.

The best time to learn to control anger is before it happens. This means tending to the false beliefs that form the embers of anger lying beneath the surface. Those thoughts and beliefs usually involve a spot that is already sore, a previous wound. For example, you may be insecure about your looks. Then, at a family gathering, your aunt jokingly comments about your less-than-perfect feature. Even worse, she compares you to the cousin who does not have your particular trait. That unflattering remark or social slight serves as the gasoline-soaked newspaper thrown onto the embers of your insecurity. Ask the Lord to heal you in those sore areas. Know who you are apart from your imperfections. Live in the depth of your identity in Christ, my friend, not in the world's shallow standards.

Angry people tend to think they have something to prove. They often answer questions nobody is asking. Everything feels like an attack on their abilities and reputation. For example, if you were poor growing up, and someone makes a remark that seems to imply you cannot afford something. Why do you need to prove you can afford it? You don't. Often, angry people work overtime to hide a weakness no one suspects they have. Does this describe you? Angry people live in fear of being hurt so they treat everyone like a suspect.

Do you struggle to control anger? In James 1:19, God says to "be quick to listen, slow to speak, and slow to get angry." Breathe. Take a step back. Get all the facts before you say anything. Remind yourself of what is true in that moment versus what your feelings say is true. Feelings are not facts. Pray for wisdom and discernment. In the Person of the Holy Spirit, you have a built-in counselor and thermostat to control your anger. Every day you expose yourself to the truth of the

God's Word, you are addressing our anger. You are crucifying the flesh and taking captive lies that are itching for a fight. As Christ conforms you to His image, you will learn to respond to anger in the way He would respond.

Controlling your anger begins before the situation arises. This includes putting on what the Bible calls the armor of God.

> Stand firm then, with the belt of truth buckled around your waist, with the breastplate of righteousness in place, and with your feet fitted with the readiness that comes from the gospel of peace. In addition to all this, take up the shield of faith, with which you can extinguish all the flaming arrows of the evil one. Take the helmet of salvation and the sword of the Spirit, which is the word of God. Ephesians 6:14-17

The following is a line-by-line of how to fight sinful anger with the armor or God.

Helmet of Salvation

The helmet protects your brain: the control center of your body. It is the most important piece of
armor in your battle against anger. Salvation affirms you; anger threatens you. Anger says you have something to prove, but salvation says you are already accepted. It says Christ makes you complete. You do not rely on the opinions of others to fulfill you. This knowledge frees you from the rabid rush of anger whenever someone tries to trigger you.

Breastplate of Righteousness

Sinful anger is founded in self-righteousness. When people

ruffle its feathers, it is ready to fight. True righteousness is in Christ, and it trumps any righteousness you construct on your own. Because Christ clothes you with His righteousness, you have nothing to prove. Your energy does not need to be spent justifying yourself. Christ already justified you. When you stop fighting other people, you discover the real battle is against your own flesh. You will start to see your need to adopt the meekness of Christ. This is strength under control.

Shield of Faith

Anger wants nothing to do with faith because it believes only in itself. Faith requires belief in someone else, which means relinquishing control. Satan is strategic. He insists that faith means weakness. If he convinces you not to believe, when your pride flairs up, you'll be back to defending yourself. The shield of faith is a water hose of truth quenching every fiery lie. It opens endless possibilities for victory. Faith invites God into your battle against anger. It gives you the humility to let God do your fighting. It shows you how to fight God's way, with weapons like love, respect, and patience toward those who trigger you (2 Corinthians 10:4).

Belt of Truth

Anger thrives on the fertilizer of lies. It says you must wear whatever labels people stick on you or fight to the death to rip them off. The truth is you don't have to do either. Anger says you are responsible for controlling what others think of you. The truth is what others think of you is none of your concern. Anger is an instigator, playing vivid clips of your opponent's beliefs about you and what you must do to stop it. The truth tells you what is real, not what is perceived. As part of your armor, the belt keeps loose clothing from getting in your way or being a tripping hazard. In your battle against anger, Jesus is the Truth that holds you together and keeps you from tripping on anything hindering your self-control.

Sword of the Spirit Which Is the Word of God

While the shield of faith is a defensive weapon, the sword of the Spirit is an offensive one. It is the most powerful tool in your arsenal against anger. It does not take your side or that of your opponent. It tells both of you what to do! The sword will correct you if you are wrong and support you when you are right. It will give you instruction in every situation (2 Timothy 3:16-17).

Anger is like an unruly child who needs discipline. The Word of God provides that discipline. Learn from it even before a fight starts. Let it strengthen you on the off-days, and you will not be caught off guard when drama calls your name. The Word of God is the wisdom of God. It will protect you from rash decisions anger suggests. His Word will prepare you for the fool who begs for a fight. It will show you when to speak and when to be quiet.

Gospel of Peace

Anger brings a fight, but the gospel brings peace. A soldier with no shoes is not prepared, no matter what else he is wearing. The gospel is the good news that Jesus Christ came into the world to save sinners. As a Christian, this is your primary message. How can anyone believe the gospel brings peace if your anger is all they see? There is more at stake than your reputation, my friend. Your anger can blind people from seeing the goodness of God in your life. Let the gospel of peace create a peaceful spirit in you. It does not make you a doormat or a pushover. It makes you a strong, spirit-filled, spirit-controlled soldier who recognizes her battle is not against people. It is a battle against an unseen enemy who wants to bring reproach on Christ's name through your anger. Forgive. It is one of the most peace-making things you will ever do. Forgiveness is the message of the gospel. The gospel of peace is your armor. It enables you to walk through sticky situations and come out with your testimony intact.

Each morning, mentally dress yourself in each piece of armor. Prepare yourself for whatever you may face each day by praying God helps you meet each incident with grace and strength.

Additional Help with Anger

Some people are more prone to anger than others, but we all have the call to control angry feelings. When you feel yourself losing control, you have a responsibility to protect yourself and others. Distance and time are great diffusers. Swallow your pride and walk away. Find healthy ways to relieve the pressure of anger. Physical or verbal assault are never right. Consider asking for help from a counselor who can provide healthy methods to gain control. Asking for help is not weakness. Maturity realizes its own limitations. Seeking guidance is one of the strongest things an angry person can do. Also, surround yourself with friends who are peace-loving. A friend who enjoys stoking your anger is not a healthy friend. Consider setting boundaries in those kinds of relationships.

Reflections

1. Which part of the armor of God do you find most helpful to fight against sinful anger?

. . .

2. How can James 1:19 aid your fight to stay calm when you're angry?

3. What lies of the devil has this chapter revealed to you about your triggers to anger?

5

Insecurity

"AND YOU ARE COMPLETE IN HIM" (Colossians 2:10). To be insecure is to experience doubt about where to put your full trust. You could lean on people, but eventually they will die, disappoint, desert, or even divorce you. In response, you might resolve to lean only on yourself. Our culture champions those who act like they don't need anybody else. You may realize, too late, this is not as solid a foundation as you hope. You discover your strength is not a match for the storms of life. You need a refuge. You cannot always be that for yourself. You try to outsmart insecurity when you trust objects like money, land, houses, and other possessions. Money can be stolen. Houses can burn down. Land is vulnerable to flood and disease. Nothing under the sun is a permanent foundation.

Where then, can you go for security? How can you feel secure when everything eventually lets you down? You must look up, my friend. God offers His sufficiency for your deficiency. He provided the cross for your insecurity. How can you doubt your worth to Him when He gave His life for you? On top of that, He gives you His Spirit, the seal of salvation only given to His spiritual children (Ephesians 1:13; Romans 8:9).

He also provides you a specific purpose no one else can fulfill (Ephesians 2:10). Does insecurity make sense in the face of all He has accomplished for you?

If you are insecure about your looks, He reminds you that you bear His image. Outer beauty only matters to those who do not understand kingdom priorities. You are unique. When you operate with this in mind, your beauty shows.

If you are insecure about measuring up to cultural standards: living in certain zip codes, bra sizes, bank account balances, and "likes" on social media, God has you covered. He says to throw it all out and use His measuring stick, instead. The world's standards of worth will be like fake money from a board game. Be rich in mercy and abound in love. This is the currency of God's kingdom.

People incite insecurity when they claim you are inherently worthless. Abusers say this to keep you under their control. Racists declare you to be inferior, despite your shared humanity. Politicians imply inequality when they deny certain groups their inalienable rights. You have little or no control of how others see you. However, you can choose whether to believe what they say. Be intentional to educate yourself about who you are in Christ and walk in that truth, my friend.

I was familiar with insecurity all throughout grade school. I was the wrong color, the wrong gender, from the wrong neighborhood, or had the wrong personality. I was depressed because I allowed others to define my worth. The first time I heard God loves me and takes pride in me, I was afraid to believe it. I was scared that somehow, I misunderstood what I heard. So, I was cautious to believe I matter to God. Sure, He died on the cross for me, but I assumed I was just lucky to be lumped in with everyone else. It was a group rate, not something specific to me. I operated from this belief for years. However, it encouraged me to be around Christians who saw my value even if I could not. They loved me, respected me, and were kind enough to meet my needs. It felt good. Then, I changed churches and encountered people who measured me by the world's standards. I became inferior again. I did not fit in anymore. After experiencing Christian love for so long, it hurt. I was in my thirties and desperate to know what to do with those feelings. I began to study the Word to settle my insecurity for the last time. If God said I was inferior, then I would learn to live with it. However, if what I heard about His love was correct, then I was ready to drink it in like a flower in the desert. My first true knowledge of the love of God came when I read 1 Peter 1:18-19. According to the passage, I was not redeemed with silver or gold, but with something far more precious: the blood of Christ. It took my breath away. My wilted spirit bloomed at the thought that I mattered enough to God for Him to pay a price higher than gold for me. It made me love Him. In the past, I only feared Him. I joined a ladies' Bible study and learned about Ephesians 1 concerning all the "in Christ" phrases that applied to me. Slowly my inner slump straightened into a confident stance of one who knew her worth to the One who made her. Around that time, I received another snub from a church member. It stung. I did not go all the way back into my slump, but I grew weary. I asked God to show me a way to hold onto the knowledge of my identity in Him. I was tired of the long recovery period every time I was criticized. One day, as I was reading Romans 8:17, God told me because I received His Son, I am His child. I already knew that, but then I read that I am an heir. Wait, I'm an heiress. I had no idea what I inherited, but I was more excited that I was God's treasure. Then, the image of a crown came to mind. That was it! As a daughter of God, I was His heiress, and I had a crown on my head. Nobody could see it, but I knew it was there. The next time somebody looked down on me, I would hold my head up, because I did not want to let my crown slip. That crown always serves to remind me I belong to Somebody, and He loves me more than gold or silver. If you are in Christ, you belong to Him, too. It takes time to let this truth sink in, but it makes all the difference in how you see yourself.

Reflections

1. What do you feel insecure about the most?

2. What is one truth in God's word that takes the sting out of your insecurity?

3. Have you found a way to keep that truth at the front of your mind? If not, what way would serve you well? A poster? A word on your bathroom mirror? Be creative! Changing a mindset takes time. Post as many reminders as you can. Write your ideas below.

6

Jealousy

JEALOUSY IS NOT HARMLESS. It destroys relationships and spreads the poison of self-centeredness. Jealousy reduces a person to an object, a desired physical feature, a bank account, or other non-eternal things. It reeks of entitlement and a worldly understanding of what matters most in life. Show me a jealous heart and I will show you where idols live.

Jealousy can be a red flag warning you where false beliefs lurk. I will use Cain, one of Adam and Eve's children, as a case study (Genesis 4). God told Cain and Abel to bring an offering. God rejected Cain's offering but accepted Abel's. God told Cain what changes to make to receive acceptance. Instead of obeying God, Cain responded to the rejection by killing his brother. Instead of taking his anger out on God for the rejection, he took it out on Abel for doing a better job. Did Cain care more about his pride than doing the right thing? Was he more concerned by his brother's triumph than receiving God's favor? Jealousy revealed his false belief that there was no room for do-overs. He wanted perfection on the first try because he was the firstborn son. Cain's reasoning may sound silly, but I encourage you to ask God to search your heart. Do not put it past your sinful nature to have silly or selfish justifications for jealousy. This can be a painful exercise, but remember God does not reveal ugliness to condemn, but to purify. His presence is the safest place to air your dirty laundry. He saw it all before you did and responded with the love of the cross.

Take Responsibility

"So the LORD said to Cain, 'Why are you angry? And why has your countenance fallen? If you do well, will you not be accepted? And if you do not do well, sin lies at the door. And its desire is for you, but you should rule over it,'" Genesis 4:6-7).

Cain was angry God rejected his offering, but accepted that of his brother, Abel. God's response to Cain reveals the characteristic He wants you to adopt to defeat jealousy: personal responsibility. God told Cain if he acted as Abel did, he would receive the same approval. In every case of jealousy, there exists an opportunity to take ownership of your actions. Instead of harboring anger because of what other people accomplish, why not seek their advice so you can emulate it? What valuable information can you learn to bring your goals closer to fulfillment? If God is the giver of every good and perfect gift, then the people you feel jealous toward are recipients of His favor. As such, you are wise to tap into those gifts if possible. Nobody can have everything they hope for, but consider what might be available to you if you give God authority over your life and destiny? No one can take what God intends for you, my friend. You are not in competition with anyone but yourself. Jealousy drains the energy God intends you to use toward running your race. When someone else reaches a goal you had for yourself, see it as a roadmap instead of an indictment against your worth or ability.

. . .

Respect Heaven's Calculator

Jealousy operates from a mindset that is not anchored in reality. To illustrate, I'll use a character called Ms. Jay. She believes everything should be equal for everyone. Ms. Jay does not apply this math when she is the one with the goods, only when someone else has what she wants. Ms. Jay revels in the jealousy of others when they long for her possessions. She does not recognize that God, the owner of all things, has the right to distribute as He sees fit. She believes the world revolves around her interests and any hindrance to this is against the will of God. If confronted, she would deny it. Her words betray the attitude of her heart when she sees inequalities in the things that matter to her. Kingdom thinking recognizes God as the Giver of all good things. His wisdom and sovereignty decide what goes to whom. Unfortunately, sin has marred the kind of equality that would eliminate need. Jealousy begrudges the blessing God allows to fall on others.

Activate Gratitude

Jealousy is the spiritual spoiled brat in all of us. When we hear about the good God gives someone instead of us, jealousy shouts, "but what about me?" Even if we are happy for the person who receives the blessing, our sinful nature struggles to keep our hearts from desiring the same thing. I know firsthand how quickly this messy emotion can suffocate the joy I have for other people's blessings.

Gratitude is the attitude that stamps out jealousy. It changes your focus from what you do not have to what you do have. It turns your eyes toward God's generosity and brings selfishness to its knees. You can't stop there. Gratitude is more than itemizing your blessings. It is recognizing how little you deserve them. This may sound like negativity, but it is a magnifying look at the grace of God. When you recognize how neither you nor your neighbor deserve any good thing, you stop measuring your blessings against theirs. You appreciate the abundance God has given you compared to what you are entitled to, which is nothing.

Exercise Contentment

What if the object of your jealousy is not within your reach? What if you are jealous of the generational wealth in your neighbor's family or your friend's beauty? Perhaps your jealous frustration stems from how easily academics come to your classmate, when you must work twice as hard. Does your sister make friends more easily than you do because she has a charismatic way about her?

Anything that is outside your control must be met with one attitude: contentment. Take inventory of your good qualities and be thankful for them. If you really want to grow, thank God for what He has given to other people, knowing that their gifts in no way diminish yours.

Notice that God's command to be content stems from His sufficiency in your life. "Be content with what you have because God has said, 'Never will I leave you, never will I forsake you '" (Hebrews 13:5b). You can be content because anything you lack is made up for by God!

Reflections

1. It is not always easy to admit jealousy. What feeling can you admit from your heart about what God has given to someone else and not to you?

. . .

2. What do you have to be thankful for? What is on your list of blessings beyond the material things?

3. When you see more fully the holiness of God, what response do you have toward Him because of what He has given you?

4. Jealousy shows where are idols are hidden. In reality, God wants to do for you what you believe something else will do. What idols might be buried in your heart?

5. Write a prayer to surrenders these idols to God. Ask God to help you see Him more fully so the idols can be disarmed.

6. Contentment is like a muscle. The more you exercise it, the stronger it grows. I have to tell myself, "Now, Georgia, you cannot have everything you want in this life. I know you want _____, but if God decides it is not in your best interest, then you do not want it anyway." I have not come to that realization overnight. At a time when I received enough of what I thought I wanted, it almost ruined me. I learned nothing is good unless it comes from God. Now I pray, asking God to quiet my flesh and help me to be content with what He has given.

7

Guilt and Shame

SHE WAS CONSUMED with passion with someone not her husband when the doors burst open. The spiritual leaders of her community dragged her out by her hair and hastily covered her with a bedsheet. She knew this was the day she would be stoned to death. She resisted hysterically as they hauled her across the cold tiles of the temple floor, her screams bouncing off the hallowed walls. The men threw her at the feet of Jesus. Sobbing with fear and shame, she dared not look up as the scribes and Pharisees shouted her crime for all to hear. Imagine her shock when Jesus did not address her, but her accusers, "Let any one of you who is without sin be the first to throw a stone at her." Through her tears, she saw Jesus bend down and write something on the ground. As he wrote, the religious leaders left the temple one by one until there was no one left. Then the Savior addressed her, "Woman, where are they? Has no one condemned you?" Wiping the tears away, she shook her head and answered, "No one, sir." Jesus then assured her He does not condemn her either. He tells her to go and sin no more. (Scripture and paraphrase from John 8:3-11).

The One who had every right to condemn her did not. This is a beautiful picture of the grace God extends to you in the face of your guilt and shame, my friend.

When I thought about what I considered my worst sins, I did not think Jesus was there offering grace and forgiveness to me. He wanted to be there, but I refused to let Him enter. I ran from Him because I was so aware of my unworthiness. Oh, I was going to church regularly, and I was reading my Bible. I was even memorizing Scripture, but I was afraid to let anything I read or heard touch the rotting guilt in my soul. I only had head knowledge of Jesus' forgiveness the day I repented and received salvation. I mechanically acknowledged the forgiveness, but I could not embrace it fully. In weaker moments, I berated myself for my past. I was afraid God would deny me certain privileges in life to punish me. When terrible things happened, I was sure God was getting back at me. The guilt hardened into shame, and I did not know how to break free.

One day, I joined a home Bible study group. I was attending for someone else's benefit, but soon realized God had some important news for me. The Bible study leader said when we refuse to embrace full forgiveness from God, it is an act of pride. That hit me hard. She explained we are saying our sin overpowers the cross's ability to atone for it. I certainly did not want to be guilty of that. I also took a hard look at my sins and saw them for what they were. The love of Christ enabled me to do it. Like sunglasses that protect eyes from sun damage, seeing my sin through the lens of grace softened the glare. The condemnation I felt melted away, and I entered a new level of intimacy with Jesus. My worship became more passionate. My love for His Word deepened. Guilt robs us of joy. Shame wants to etch itself into our souls. We can over-come both with the truth of God's mercy and grace.

What sin have you carried too long? In what ways have

you allowed your past to condemn you? It is time to silence the condemning voices you have heard for so long.

Guilt points out the wrong you have done. It is God's gift to alert you when you violate His boundaries. His desire is never to condemn you. He desires you make the necessary corrections. How do you move from condemnation to correction?

Acknowledgement

First, God calls you to acknowledge wrong. Make no mistake, He knows your sin, your guilt, and your shame. He does not ignore it or accept excuses for it. Christ saw that the woman caught in adultery was not denying her guilt. Sometimes the human heart has an amazing capacity for denial. The woman could have said her accusers were lying. She could have pointed to their motives to frame Jesus and distract from her own guilt. She could have cursed the crowd, saying what she did in private was none of their business. If these excuses were the stance of her heart, Jesus would have addressed it. Because He did not, it is presumed she did not deny her sin. Jesus invites you and I to confess our own guilt before Him. Resist the urge to put on the robe of forgiveness before taking a bath of humble confession, my friend. An unwashed conscience makes for a stinky, entitled, and arrogant attitude. It says to God, "Of course Christ forgives me," before saying, "Christ have mercy on me for my filthy sin!" The brutality of the cross showed God's attitude toward your sin. Never let that be lost in the face of God's grace. You cannot appreciate mercy until you know how little you deserve it. This is not wallowing, but awareness.

It is uncomfortable to look at our poor choices and rebellion. Skipping to the forgiveness part before introspection is a fast-track to doing the same wrong again. Coming so close to death by stoning was a powerful deterrent for the adulterous woman, but the grace in Christ's voice topped that. Grace is disarming and it provokes love and loyalty no stone or whip ever could.

Repentance

Repentance is the next step. Because this is about your relationship with God, how can anything be right if you have no intention of turning from your sin? There is no reconciliation if the adulterer refuses to leave her partner. You have further confessing to do if you have no desire to leave your sin. Jesus stands ready to hear you on this.

You may not trust yourself to stay true to a promise not to return to sin. This is understandable. However, when you realize you are not the one with the power to overcome sin, you can repent with more confidence. Ask the Lord to live His life through you. Tap into the power you already possess in the person of the Holy Spirit. This is not a one and done exercise. Daily surrender yourself to His lordship and have regular accountability to others. Over time, you will see victory in areas that once were strongholds.

Acceptance

Once you confess and repent, acceptance of God's forgiveness, cleansing, and grace are in order. When your guilt is severe, you may struggle to accept that God forgives you. You may flog yourself spiritually by repeating how undeserving you are. If you already confessed, then pride may be standing in the way of true repentance. Your sin is no worse than anyone else's, my friend. Pride says your sin requires self-punishment and groveling. Your spiritual adversary wants to prolong confession and keep you from enjoying what Christ paid so much for you to have. Accept God's forgiveness as fact so you can get on with living out your purpose. Part of accepting freedom from guilt is rejoicing. Praise God for how good He is and hail Him with hallelujahs for His great cleansing.

None of the above steps need to be long and drawn out. Just make sure you do not skip any of them. The praise part will never end as you daily itemize His blessings of forgiveness.

Shame can be a feeling and an identity. The feeling part can be embarrassment or humiliation when you contemplate what you have done. As with guilt, accepting what shame says you did is part of the confession process and can be healthy.

No excuses.

No deflecting.

Just acceptance.

The identity part of shame is a different story. Shame says you *are* what you did. It attacks your identity and condemns you. Jesus has a lot to say about this lie. I address this more in-depth in the chapter on insecurity, but for now, know that when you received Christ, you became a new creation (2 Corinthians 5:17). He no longer sees you as condemned. He took condemnation away. "Therefore there is now no condemnation for those who are in Christ Jesus" (Romans 8:1). You were given a new spiritual DNA. You are no longer who or what you were before. When you do what your sin nature desires, you are a new creation doing what your old self did, but you are not what you did. Know this! Believe this!

Reflections

To be human is to be guilty, to fall short of God's perfect standard. To receive the mercy of God through the work of Jesus on the cross is to be redeemed and declared guiltless. To be free is to live in the truth of forgiveness and cleansing. It also means life is about having gratitude for forgiveness, not trying to earn it.

What will you do with the guilt you feel? Maybe it is time to write a declaration in agreement with what God says about your guilt and shame. Below is a suggested declaration, but you may write your own.

Declaration of Freedom from Guilt and Shame

> *Because I have trusted Jesus Christ as my Lord and Savior, I*
> *,_____ declare, in agreement with God, I am no*
> *longer under condemnation. I declare I am free from guilt because*
> *Christ paid what I owe to God through His perfect blood. I declare I*
> *am free from shame because Christ has given me a new identity. He*
> *calls me blameless, forgiven, and set free from anything or anyone laying*
> *blame at my feet. I am His child now. Today, I choose to allow Christ*
> *to live His life through me while I learn to surrender daily to His will,*
> *and not my own. Amen!*
>
> Signed and dated _____

You may want to copy and frame this declaration. This is an important moment in your life when you decided to believe God's forgiveness and no longer live under the weight of guilt or shame. It also helps to tell someone about your new start. I would love to be one of those people. You may email me at Georgia@encouragementoutpost.com to share this good news.

8

Worry And Anxiety

WORRY AND ANXIETY are a natural response when you realize something is outside your control. Your teenager driving for the first time without you, your elderly mother living alone in another state, or a friend battling addiction re-enters normal life after a stretch in rehab. All of these situations can provoke anxiety. You know you should not worry, but how do you stop?

Philippians 4:6-7 says, "Do not be anxious about anything, but in every situation, by prayer and petition, with thanksgiving, present your requests to God. And the peace of God, which transcends all understanding, will guard your hearts and your minds in Christ Jesus." I will dissect these two verses to encourage you toward victory over worry.

Do not be anxious about anything

I once visited a friend in Singapore. This Asian country is famous for its strict laws about litter as well as its fines for every little infraction. My friend was one step ahead of me on the escalator as we descended. I noticed a tiny leaf, about a half inch long, nestled in her hair. As I plucked it out, I intended to flick it into the air, not considering where it might land. My friend stopped me and immediately held out her palm for me to hand her the leaf. She must have seen my surprise. I thought it ridiculous that she was so careful not to allow even a miniscule leaf to touch the ground. She explained that someone was always watching, and I could incur a hefty fine for littering, even something as small as that leaf. Singapore had a zero-tolerance policy on littering. God says you are to have a zero-tolerance policy for worry taking up space in your heart. You and I are not to worry about the little things, even as small as that leaf. No worrying is allowed about the big things either. None. This is hard to do, is it not?

But in every situation, by prayer and petition

God does not only tell us not to worry. He tells you what to do instead. He says to pray. Pray about everything. I once heard a friend say she only prays about the big things. She does not wish to bother God with the little things, since He has so much to do. The God who said to pray about everything meant what He said. Can you think of anyone else who has so much to do? He keeps the planets in line and still helps you find your car keys. The sheer magnitude of who God is should free you to hurl every need onto His capable shoulders.

In Helen M. Young's encouraging book, *Mary Hollingsworth's Love Notes from God: Inspirational Messages from God's Heart to Yours*, I read a beautiful account of a British missionary named Helen Roseveare who served as a nurse in Zaire, Africa (now, the Congo). Helen was working all night to assist in the birth of a baby, only for the mother to die shortly after. The mother left not only a newborn, but a two-year-old daughter crying with grief too big for her little heart. Though Zaire is on the equator, its nighttime chill can be a death sentence for a newborn. Helen sent her assistant to get a hot water bottle to place in the box where the infant slept. Horror filled the assistant's eyes as she told Helen the water bottle had burst. It was the last one. Rubber erodes quickly in the dry African climate. There were no drug stores or electricity, so they needed to build a fire to save the baby. Stoking the flames, Helen wrapped the baby in cotton wool and assigned the assistant with the singular task of helping the baby survive the night. She laid the baby as close to the fire as she dared and used her own body as a barrier against the treacherous draft coming in under the door.

The next day, Helen told the children at the orphanage about the infant. She asked them to pray for the baby's survival. One of the children, Ruth, volunteered to lead the group in prayer that morning. Helen's mouth jaw dropped at Ruth's blunt request that God send the needed hot water bottle that day. It would be no use to send it later because the baby would be dead by then. The missionary admitted in her heart she did not believe the request would be granted. She reasoned the only way for a hot water bottle to arrive that day would be if it came in the mail. She had been serving there four years. Not once had she gotten anything from back home. Ruth was not finished, though. She asked that God also send a little doll for the baby's big sister so that she would know she is loved by God. Helen struggled to say, "Amen," behind such a bold prayer. Finishing her daily rounds at the makeshift clinic, Helen arrived home and found a package on her doorstep. Tears stung her eyes. She knew she must take the package back to the orphanage to open in front of the children. The orphans all watched as Helen untied the string on the box. From the top of the box, she pulled out some jerseys knitted by a group of ladies back home. Next were some bandages for leprosy patients. Then some raisins. As soon as she felt something rubbery, she knew what it was: the hot water bottle! Eyes dancing with joy, Ruth ran to the box and exclaimed that if God had sent the hot water bottle, He had also sent the doll she requested of Him. Sure enough, out came a doll from the bottom of the box. Helen burst into tears, realizing God must have spoken to the hearts of a group of women back home five months prior. Following the prompting of His Spirit, one of the women packed a hot water bottle, an unlikely gift for folks living so close to the equator. God also knew a little two-year-old would need the comfort of a little doll that looked just like her. He knew a baby would need a hot water bottle to survive, and it needed to arrive on the day Ruth requested. Little Ruth prayed for the big and the small. You and I must too.

Pray about everything, my friend. Pray for a good parking spot. Pray God helps you find your keys or your phone. Pray for your spouse to have a good relationship with coworkers. Pray about important things, trivial things, and everything-in-between things.

Notice the verse says to *pray* about everything. Instead, sometimes we talk to friends about it, research it, think about it, and complain about it. Be intentional to pray about it!

Present Your Requests to God

You may think this is just another statement about praying. However, it contains a crucial element God wants you to remember. Imagine a number "1" written on a board. It is not just a straight, vertical line, but it has room for a child to color the inside. Now, picture a request you have for God, like blessing your child as he goes off to college. The biblical language translated "requests" refers to a single object made up of many parts. So, your single request to have your child be blessed should be made up of many specific parts. Inside that number "1" you would list several blessings you want for your child going off to college. What specific ways do you want God to bless him? You want protection when he drives, wisdom in choosing friends, favor with the professors, diligence in study, and so on. That is what it means to make requests known to God. It means to pray specifically. Itemize in prayer, my friend!

With Thanksgiving

Whenever you pray, do not neglect giving thanks. Why? Giving thanks puts your faith on hyperdrive. As you thank God for what He has already done, your faith increases. It is easier to believe that He will answer future requests. It is impossible to please God without faith, so always apply thanksgiving. It is the fertilizer for future blessing.

The peace of God, which transcends all understanding will guard your hearts

God has His own brand of peace. It is the kind that makes no logical sense, and you cannot get it anywhere else. When you pray, God exchanges your anxiety for His peace. He promises when you pray thoroughly, specifically, and thankfully, His peace will result.[1]

Reflections

Which of the above do you struggle most in worry? Do you see the need to pray more specifically? Are you sparse in the giving of thanks? Do you pray for the little requests but find you are too overwhelmed to pray about the big needs?

List one specific request on your heart these days. Write a detailed list of the ways you are asking God to answer that need.

---

1. Mary Hollingsworth, *Love Notes from God: Inspirational Messages from God's Heart to Yours (Love Notes, 2)* (Illinois: Tyndale House Publishers, 2003), 81-86.

Call to Action

YOU ARE AN EMOTIONAL BEING. Your emotions are a gift of God providing a valve to release and process the happenings of life. They are also a means of expressing worship to God. Sin has marred your emotions, but because of Christ's power in you, you can reclaim control of them. This process will last a lifetime, and you must determine to submit it to the lordship of Christ. Your emotions are a beautiful expression of who you are and how you view life. Messy emotions spill onto everyone you encounter. Emotions come with an aroma. Do you want to smell like a skunk or like refreshing perfume? Emotions are connected to important thoughts and beliefs. Allow Christ to tackle your selfish and false beliefs. Then, you will emit His fragrance of love and service to others. When you make a mistake and express your emotions poorly, humble yourself. Rejoice when Christ enables you to express yourself lovingly.

Reading God's Word is like looking in a spiritual mirror. How often do you look in that mirror? God's Word will correct you, rebuke you, encourage you, and conform you until you live and talk like Jesus. Keep an ongoing dialogue with Jesus through prayer. This gives Him opportunities to give you gentle correction and pat you on the back when you do well. Also, regularly spend time around a community of like-minded Christians. This will give you the context in which to grow. "As iron sharpens iron, so one man sharpens another." (Proverbs 27:17). Good friends will help you on your journey to being like Jesus. Finally, if you want to learn to handle your messy emotions, commit your heart to do so. Change is hard, but possible. It will not happen automatically. You must be intentional about allowing Christ to reflect Himself through you. You must decrease so that He will increase. You are a beautiful creation. You have incredible and significant gifts to offer the world. Submit your beautiful self to Christ daily and let His light shine through you in the pattern only you possess, my friend. Let Him "un-mess" those messy emotions and radiate the fruit of His Spirit.

Index

HOW TO BECOME A CHRISTIAN

GOD LOVES YOU SO MUCH, my friend (John 3:16). He showed this love the best when He solved the biggest problem you have (Romans 5:8). That problem is that you are a sinner (Romans 3:23). Your sin separates you from God, and God wants you back. The only way for that to happen was for someone innocent to bear the punishment for your sin. God cannot let sin go unpunished. Jesus Christ was the only One qualified to bear that punishment because He was innocent (2 Corinthians 5:21). When He died on the cross, He took the punishment your sins deserve, and now you have the opportunity to be free from guilt (John 3:18)! Salvation is not automatic just because Christ died for you. You must decide to receive this amazing gift by faith (John 1:12). Faith requires putting your full trust in what Christ did on the cross for you and acknowledging Him as Lord of your life. He said, "I am the way and the truth and the life. No one comes to the Father except through me" (John 14:6). Surrender any other ways you have tried to receive forgiveness from God. No other way will work (Acts 4:12). Salvation is not a reward to be earned, it is a gift of grace to be received (Ephesians 2:8-9). What a gift!

If you have never received God's gift of salvation, you can do it right now. Pray a prayer of surrender to Christ as your only hope. Ask Him to forgive all your sins based on what Christ did on the cross. Then, thank Him for keeping His promise to save you (John 6:47).

If you just received Christ's gift of salvation by faith for the first time, I would love to know. You may share your salvation story with me at Georgia@encouragementoutpost.com.

About the Author

Dr. Georgia Pointer's vision is to encourage as many people as she can in their walk with Christ. Wherever darkness of sorrow, fear, or discouragement exists around her, her passion is to shine the light of Christ. Overcoming so much of what this book is about, she delights to show others how to find healing for every hurt. She firmly believes every hurt can be healed through an intimate relationship with Jesus Christ and by the power of His Word. God placed His light within her when she united with Christ as a teenager. Many individuals invested in Georgia and taught her what it means to follow Jesus. God gave her examples and knowledge of His Word.

Georgia received her Bachelor of Arts degree in Biblical Studies at Blue Mountain College in Mississippi. Years later, she received a Master of Christian Education degree from Mid-America Baptist Theological Seminary in Memphis, Tennessee. She also earned a Ph.D. in Christian Counseling through Cornerstone University in Louisiana.

Georgia's ministry of encouragement includes serving as a counselor in a recovery facility and a pregnancy center. She also writes and teaches women's Bible studies. Her devotional blog, EncouragmentOutpost.com, seeks to encourage women to have a biblical perspective on their struggles. She enjoys speaking at retreats and conferences. She also enjoys reading and making quilts. She is married to Keith and they both raised and homeschooled three sons.

CPSIA information can be obtained
at www.ICGtesting.com
Printed in the USA
JSHW040202180822
29383JS00003B/13

9 798985 413007